25 WAYS
TO IMPROVE
YOUR LIFE

H. H. SRI SRI RAVI SHANKAR

25 Ways to Improve Your Life

1st edition: March 2010
2nd edition: May 2010

Printed in India by Jwalamukhi Mudranalaya Pvt. Ltd., Bangalore
Ph: +91-80-26601064, 26617243

ISBN 978-938059232-9

THE ART OF LIVING

Sri Sri Publications Trust,
Art of Living International Centre,
21st KM, Kanakapura Road, Udayapura, Bangalore - 560 082
Phone: 080-32722473
Email: info@srisripublications.com
Website: store.artofliving.org

TABLE OF CONTENTS

Transform
yourself

- H. H. Sri Sri Ravi Shankar

$\mathscr{I}$n this era of science and technology, we can be creative and productive, and at the same time not lose the humanness that we are all born with. Just material things or comfort alone do not make you comfortable. You may have a good bed to sleep on, but unable to sleep because of insomnia or worry! You need to get a broad understanding about yourself and your priorities. Clarity in the mind makes things much easier. Understanding your basic emotions like love, your interaction with people around you, knowing about your ego or what your intellect or mind is saying to you and introspection will give you a few minutes of relaxation which is very vital. So, what is most important is introspection about one's own life and how to improve the quality of life. This intention itself will open many doors for you to feel better about yourself. First of all, find out for yourself whether you are healthy.

Health is...

A disease-free body.
A quiver-free breath.
A stress-free mind.
An inhibition-free intellect.
An obsession-free memory.
An ego that includes all.
A soul that is free from sorrow.

Have you ever thought

1. What is the purpose of your life?

2. What is the meaning of life?

3. What is life all about?

These questions are very, very precious. When these questions dawn in your mind, only then your life begins! But, when these questions come into your mind, don't be in a hurry to get an answer. Those who know will not tell you and those who tell; don't know! You can plug your ears and walk off! These questions are the tools by which you can dig deeper and the answers come from within you. Once these questions come into your life then you start "living" life rather than just existing. To know for what you are on this planet, find out what you are not here for!

- You are not here to be sad.
- You are not here to blame.
- You are not here to be miserable.
- You are not here to worry.
- You are not here to show off.
- You are not here to get stressed out.
- You are not here to get irritated and irritate others.
- The list goes on. . . . .

THE ART OF LIVING

*A*ll our struggles in life is to know more. You are trying your level best to understand your feelings and emotions, and you get into more and more and more confusion. This is what has happened with psychology today. It tries to explain to you why you feel like the way you are feeling. The 'why' arises always when you are unhappy. You ask "Why this problem to me of all the people?" Nobody ever asked, "Why am I so happy?" You want to understand, "Why am I not feeling good?", or "Why am I angry?", or "Why is this not happening?" The more you try to understand and try to dig in, you seem to understand less and less. The mystery deepens, an illusion comes as though "I know it". But that is for a short while. We ourselves do not know and we try to explain to others! Stop your explanations; your explanations put you into a soup and also make other people more confused. You don't know what is happening in your mind. Mind is like a roller coaster. It's a crowd. Just be in the simple and innocent state of "I don't know!". This life is a mystery- it's beautiful-live it. Living the mystery of life totally is joy. Becoming the mystery is divine. You are a mystery! When you see life in this context, clarity dawns in your mind and your life improves.

I'M A MYSTERY!

1. Review the context of your life

$\mathcal{L}$ook at your own life in the light of time. Millions of years have passed and millions will come.

What is your life? 60, 70 or 100 years? Span of life is insignificant. It is not even a drop in the ocean. In terms of space you simply don't exist! This understanding dissolves the ego. Ego is ignorance of your reality, ignorance of your existence. Now, just to know this, do we have to do something else? Just open your eyes and ask: "Who am I? How I am on this planet? What is my life time?" Awareness dawns in the mind, and you will stop worrying about little things like, "This person said this thing to me and that person broke away with me and this happened with that person and I am going to say this...." All smallness will simply drop away, and you will be able to live every moment of your life. Your life reels around your context. You should be happy in life. All other businesses involve ups and downs which is very natural. If there is a body, then it will get cold, cough, fever or something else and it will go away. But take care to see that happiness is always established in you. That is known as Purushartha. Our love, faith and belief should be deep-rooted, then everything else moves on its own. How many events take place in life! Are you able to maintain your equanimity always? Not everything in the world is sweet. If you are grounded in faith, like the husk with grain, you will progress. Take this decision, "Whatever happens I will be there. I will be grounded. God's protection is there on me. Whatever happens, I will never go down. I always have God's hand with me." Keep your mind in peace in all situations. The rest will be taken care of. You have to take at least one step forward, which is to be in peace and equanimity.

"Oh! Nothing happened. Nothing of my work happened." If you are able to laugh in such a situation, then understand that you have protection with you! The world is filled with love. Everybody has love inside them. You have to see that in your mind.

Your head will be in the mud in a few years; don't put mud in your head while you are still alive!

If you review the context of your life, the quality of your life will improve.

2. Know life's Impermanence

$\mathscr{S}$ee the impermanence in this life. That is the truth. Turn back and see that all that you did is like a dream. All have passed, the whole thing is finished. Tomorrow will pass.

Now and then, a pinch of unpleasantness comes. It makes you aware of your pleasantness. Suppose you never had unpleasant moments in life, you would never have pleasant ones. Your life would stagnate in utter boredom and you would become like a stone. So, in order to keep you alive, now and then, here and there, nature gives you a little pinch. It makes life more lively. Accept it. You don't have to be afraid in life. There is always support. So, every pinch that you are having in life is for the best, to make your life more lively and enjoyable.

Day and night you work so hard. The whole week is spent working, coming home tired, eating, going to bed. The same routine the next day. Weekends have become another routine. If you're awake, then you see there is so much foolishness! Just watch when four or five people get together and have a gossip session. In a gossip session, you can immediately change the topic of conversation. This is the thing with a crowd. If ten people are talking about the weather and you change the topic to stock markets, everybody will immediately talk stock markets, whether they know about them or not. It is great fun.

Being aware of this impermanent nature of our life, you find that there is something in you that has not changed. There is a reference point by which you can say things are changing. That reference point is the source of life. That is wisdom. With wisdom, your life improves.

3. Make your smile cheaper

A research done in England found that a baby smiles 400 times a day, an adolescent 17 times and an adult doesn't smile at all! The More successful people keep a very stiff face. Is roughness a sign of success? Is being stressed a sign of prosperity, growth or dignity?

You should smile more. Every day, every morning, look at the mirror and give a good smile to yourself. You know what happens when you smile? All the muscles in your face get relaxed. The nerves in your brain get relaxation, and you get the confidence, courage and energy to move on in life.

You know, your smile is so fragile! Just one telephone call is enough to take it away! But what is the big deal about your feelings? Bundle them up and throw them into the ocean!

Once you are rid of your 'feelings', you can be happy. Just see why your spirits go down? Because somebody said something stupid to you. And why did they say a stupid thing? Because they had some garbage they needed to throw out and you were there, ready to catch it! And once you have caught it, you hold on to it so passionately! Come on! Wake up! Don't let your smile be snatched away by anybody!

Usually, you give your anger freely and smile rarely as though a smile is costly. In ignorance, anger is cheaper and smile costly. In knowledge, a smile is free like sun, air, and water; and anger is extremely expensive, like a diamond. Make your smile cheaper and anger expensive! You are here for a greater cause. Just remember that. Take a challenge: "Come what may, I am going to smile today and be happy!" Smile more.

THE ART OF LIVING

4. Be enthusiastic and praise others

𝒞nthusiasm is the nature of life. We often have a tendency to put cold water on other's enthusiasm.

Reverse this tendency. Take every opportunity to praise others and support their enthusiasm. If you put down other's enthusiasm, the same may happen to you. As you sow, so shall you reap. Recollect how much enthusiasm and joy you had when you went to the primary school. Someone without enthusiasm is like a corpse. But as you mature, the enthusiasm curve declines. As enthusiasm declines, we stop communicating.

How would you like to see yourself ? Happy and bubbling with enthusiasm or dull and difficult to please? Often, you like to be pleased, appeased and cajoled. So you put up a tough, upset face and act difficult to please. If a person has to appease and please ten people all the time, it will be so tiring. People who keep a long face and expect others to cajole and appease them make others run away. Lovers often do this. They expend a lot of energy in cajoling, and this brings down the joy and celebration of the moment.

If you feel down, appease and please yourself. Your need to be appeased by someone else is the sign of grossness. If you want attention, all you get is tension. It is not possible to attain Divine Love with a complaining face. Become one whose enthusiasm never dies.

5. *Make meditation a part of your life*

$\mathcal{T}$he higher goals in life can only be realised through a few minutes of meditation and introspection.

What is meditation?

Mind without agitation is meditation.

Mind in the present moment is meditation.

Mind that has no hesitation, no anticipation is meditation.

Mind that has come back home, to the source, is meditation.

Mind that becomes "no mind" is meditation.

Deeper you are able to rest, dynamic you will be in activity. Even though deep rest and dynamic activity are opposite values, they are complementary. Before the body leaves you, you learn to leave everything. That is freedom. What are you looking for? Are you looking for some great joy? YOU ARE JOY!

I will give you an example. Have you seen dogs biting bones? You know why they bite bones?

Biting creates wounds in their mouth. Its own blood comes out and the dog feels that the bone is very tasty! Poor dog spends the whole time chewing the bone but getting nothing out of it! Any joy you experience in life is from the depth of your Self, when you let go all that you hold on to and settle down being centered in that space. That is called meditation. Actually, meditation is not an act; it is the art of doing nothing! The rest in meditation is deeper than the deepest sleep that you can ever have, because in meditation you transcend all desires.

Meditation is letting go of anger from the past and all the planning for the future.

Meditation is accepting this moment and living every moment totally with depth. Just this understanding, and a few days of continuous practice of meditation can change the quality of our life. The best comparison of the three states of consciousness-waking, sleeping and dreaming is with nature. Nature sleeps, awakens and dreams! It happens in a magnificent scale in existence, and it is happening in a different scale in the human body. Wakefulness and sleep are like sunrise and darkness. Dream is like the twilight in between.

And meditation is like the flight to the outer space, where there is no sunset, no sunrise, nothing!

I am sure that deep within, every one of you feel that you have not grown, meaning you have not changed, not grown old. This indicates the soul in you, the depth in you, the spirit in you doesn't change, doesn't grow old, it's not aging. The body is aging but something in you is not aging. Getting in touch with that something that doesn't age, brings beauty in life. That is meditation.

6. Go to the most beautiful place

THE ART OF LIVING

*O*nly if there is alertness and presence of mind, can your life improve. For this, you need to cultivate the habit of listening. Most of us are not good listeners. When you are listening to somebody, the speaker's very first sentence triggers some conversation within you. You are constantly agreeing or disagreeing with the speaker. Have you ever wondered whether you can listen without any thoughts or pre-conceived notions? To cultivate the habit of listening, you have to 'go' to a place where everything is beautiful!

Where is this place? That most beautiful place is within you! When you come to this place, then any place is beautiful. Then, wherever you go, you add beauty there.

Learning something about our breath is very important. Our breath has a great lesson to teach us: for every rhythm in the mind, there is a corresponding rhythm in the breath, for every rhythm in the breath, there is a corresponding emotion. So, when you cannot handle your mind directly, through breath you can handle the mind. Neither at school nor at home does anybody teach you what to do when you are upset or angry or depressed.

The first thing we did when we came to this planet is that we took a deep breath and then we started to cry. The last thing we'll be doing: we'll breathe out and make others cry! In between, the whole life, we are breathing in and out, but, we have learnt very little about our breath! No breath, no life... know breath, know life!

We need to learn a little bit about our breath. We need to know a little bit about all the layers of our existence-body, breath, mind, intellect, memory, ego and the Self. This is what I call Art of Living, learning a little bit about ourselves, the seven layers of our life.

And that makes you be in the present moment, and it helps us to maintain the innocence that we are all born with, and feel at home with everybody, anywhere. What I would suggest is, take one week off every year for yourself, like you take your car for servicing.

During that time, align yourself with nature, wake up with the sunrise, do some exercise, eat proper food, just as much food as necessary, some exercises, yoga, and some breathing exercises, a few minutes of singing, and then some silent moments, enjoying the creation.

Book yourself on a trip to this most beautiful place in the universe. Then you find that every day is a vacation and a celebration!

7. Communicate effectively

$\mathcal{L}$earning to communicate effectively with everyone is a skill worth possessing. Most of the time you find that you are out of place. Communicating without prejudice is vital for success.

If you are faced with someone who knows more than you, be like a child and keep your ears and eyes open for learning. If you are faced with someone who knows less than you, be humble and strive to make them as good as or better than you. Play with a small child as you played when you were a child. Talk with an elderly person remembering that one day you will be like that. Communicate with a person of your age group like you are his or her best friend.

This world is varied beyond our imagination, and there's always something to share, learn and teach. When you are centered, you become a powerful communicator. And when your communication improves, your life improves.

8. Take out time for yourself

$\mathcal{I}$f for the whole day you are engaged in only gathering information, you do not take out time for yourself to think and reflect. A few quiet moments are sources for creativity. Some time during the day, sit for a few minutes, get into the cave of your heart, eyes closed, and kick the world away like a ball. But, during the day be 100 per cent attached to the work. Eventually, you will be able to be both attached and detached. This is the skill of living, the art of living.

Renunciation refills your energy. Creativity cannot happen just through efforts.

There is a beautiful story about Chhatrapati Shivaji. At one time Shivaji became so frustrated about ruling his kingdom that he went to his guru Samarth Ramdas and told him that he is fed up and that he just wants to renounce everything. Ramdas told him that he can renounce everything. Shivaji became so happy and relaxed at the very thought.

Then Ramdas told him; "Now I am the king and you are my servant.

Will you do whatever I ask you to do?" Shivaji replied; "For you I am ready to do anything." Ramdas said; "Very good. Will you run this country for me?" Shivaji replied: "Yes, I will run the country for you!" Total renunciation had brought zeal and enthusiasm in him. Creativity springs up when you are relaxed. You have to renounce all work you have done the whole day, only then can you rest in the night.

Though many times pain, struggle and frustration have brought out creativity in some people, these are not the only reasons for a person to be creative. Millions of people in the world are struggling or frustrated, but they are not creative. So, taking out some time for yourself improves the quality of your life.

9. Better the world around you

A river needs two banks to flow. The difference between flood and a normal river is that water flow is regulated in a river. During floods, water has no direction. Similarly, the energy in our life needs some direction to flow. If you don't give direction, it is all confusion. Today, most people are confused because there is no direction in life. When you are happy, there is so much of life-energy in you; but when this life-energy doesn't know where to go, how to go, it gets stuck. When it stagnates, it rots. For life-energy to move in a direction, commitment is essential.

Life runs with commitment. If you observe every small thing or big thing in life, they go with certain commitment. A student takes admission in a school or college with a commitment. Needless to say, a family runs on commitment: mother is committed to the child, child is committed to the parents, husband is committed to wife, and wife is committed to husband. Greater the commitment you take, greater the energy or power you gain to fulfill that commitment.

Greater the commitment, easier things are. Smaller the commitment, more suffocating it is for you. Smaller commitments suffocate you because you have more capacity, but you are stuck in a small hole!

When you have ten things to do and if one thing goes wrong, you can keep doing the ten things; the thing that has gone wrong will set itself right! But if you have only one thing to do and that goes wrong, then you are stuck with it. Usually we think we should have resource and then we will commit. Greater the commitment you take, greater the resources will come to you automatically. Whatever you are committed to, brings you strength. If you are committed to your family then your family supports you, if you are committed to society, you enjoy the support of society. Commitment will always bring comfort in the long run. Make a commitment to make this world a better place to live.

10. Nourish your emotions

$\mathcal{A}$ person without emotions is like wood, without any juice. You need to make your life interesting to make people be with you. This will happen when you nurture yourself with music, prayer and service.

The way to expand from individual to universal consciousness is to share others' sorrow and joy. As you grow, your consciousness should also grow. When you expand in knowledge with time, then depression is not possible. The way to overcome personal misery is to share universal misery! The way to expand personal joy is to share universal joy. Instead of thinking "What about me?" and "What can I gain from this world?", think "What can I do for the world?"

Silence heals and rejuvenates. Silence gives you depth and stability and brings creativity.

Service leads to the dynamic experience of heart. It creates a sense of belongingness.

Lack of service can land a person in depression. Pain is inevitable. Suffering is optional. Pain is physical. Suffering is mental. If you are not sensitive to others' pain, then you are not a human being. That is why you need to serve. Service alone can bring contentment in life, but service without silence tires you. Service without spirituality will be shallow, and cannot be sustained for a long period. The deeper the silence, the more dynamic the outer activity. Both are essential in life.

When you bring some relief or freedom to someone through seva, good vibrations and blessings come to you. Seva brings merit; merit allows you to go deep in meditation; meditation brings back your smile. When you sing and pray from your heart , your emotions are nourished and you become lively.

11. Plan short and long-term goals

At any given point of time, our mind is oscillating between the past and the future. Either it is angry or sad about the past or anxious about the future. Whatever actions you do in this state of mind, you regret after some time. This is how you get caught up in the same old cycle. Does it mean that you should not plan your future? No! You should plan your short and long-term goals. Then, and only then, life gets a channel, a direction to flow.

When the mind is totally in the present, the right planning happens. Not only should you plan your goals, but plan the means and methods to work towards them. Where would you like to see yourself after three years? After 20 years? After 40 years? Don't be feverish about the results. Give your 100 per cent. If you are feverish about the results, it will lead you to disappointment.

Do not make a list of all the things you want to achieve. Select few things that really matters. Once a teacher brought a glass jar to the class and a bag with some big stones, some small stones and some sand. He asked the students to put all the contents from the bag into the glass jar. Some students put the sand first, then small stones and by then there was no place for the big stones. The teacher later explained that had they put the bigger stones first, then the smaller stones, there was always space around the stones for all the sand in the bag.

This example teaches us an important lesson in prioritising things. If we put things that will give us maximum fulfillment in the long term, smaller things will automatically fall into place.

Among all planets in the solar system, the earth is privileged to host life in its many forms, and among all the species, humans are most privileged, for they can host knowledge. Again and again you remember that you are peace, you are love, you are joy and that you are hosting the creator. If you do not realise that you are the host, you live like a ghost!

12. Prayer is a vital tool

$\mathcal{P}$rayer is a vital tool to improve your life. It also nurtures values like integrity and honesty. Prayer happens in two situations, or in a combination of situations. When you feel grateful or when you feel utterly helpless. If you are not grateful and prayerful, you will be miserable. In either case your prayers will be answered. What you can do, you do. What you cannot do, you pray for! It is said the divine dawns in you when you pray for it, when you cry for it, when you sing for it. The divine is only waiting for you to dig a little deeper into yourself. Because, it can then fill you with much more nectar! Divine wants you to create more space in you.

Cry from your soul for help. This is for those seekers who are weak. Those seekers who are strong with the power of knowledge can sing with that joy of what they have achieved! The moment you sing in gratitude, in glory of the divine, it immediately dawns in you, and fills you up again. One type of people are grateful for all their growth. The other type are helpless and weak. Both will be helped.

Spirituality is not some ritual, or doing something. It's a very pleasant, uplifted state of being and seeing that the whole world is all spirit or consciousness. Use prayer to bring integration in your personality. Whatever you do, know that the higher power has the final say and it will always be for the best.

13. Implement changes if needed

Sorrow simply means that 'viveka' (discrimination) is overshadowed. Viveka means knowing that everything is changing. Your body, your emotions, the people around you and the world-everything is changing. Time and again you have to awaken to this reality.

You are often fearful of change. Change is inevitable in many fronts though security is hooked on to stability. You know there is a need for change to improve your life, but you feel secure in the old pattern. You need the courage to implement changes whenever it is necessary. You have to evaluate the pros and the cons. You have to see whether something gives you short-term joy and misery in the long run or short-time pain and joy in the long run.

Life is a combination of both change and non-change. So, use your intelligence and courageously implement changes when you feel that there is a need for change.

14. Identify your limitations

$\mathcal{E}$very time you are unhappy or miserable, you are just coming in touch with your own boundaries! And what can you do? You can just feel thankful: "Oh, I came in touch with my boundary, my limitation. This was my limitation." You just turn the whole situation into a prayer: "Let there be peace, not just in me but in everybody." Prayer is that moment when you come in touch with your limitations, your boundaries.

You are peaceful, you are joyful, you are happy as long as you have not come in contact with your boundaries. At that moment what can you do? You can just say, "My Lord, my God, You made me become aware of my boundaries. You bring peace. I am giving it all to You." That very moment you will start smiling. However hopeless the situation is, you will walk through it, sing through it, dance through it! This is love.

In Hindi, love is written with two-and-a-half letters. They say, "Who is a master, who is a pundit, who is a wise person? Not one who has studied a lot of scriptures, but one who has studied the two-and-a-half letters.

It is a test of the moment, when you come in touch with your limitations, your boundaries. You are happy, peaceful. Are you in the boundaries? Or are you maintaining your boundless and the innocent love in the heart? Is it remaining? If it is, then nothing can rob you of peace.

15. Do not lose your friends

$\mathscr{M}$istakes keep happening all the time. Often you want to correct them. How much can you correct? There are two situations when you correct others' mistakes.

1 You correct someone's mistake because it bothers you. But even if you correct it, this does not work.

2 You correct someone's mistake not because it bothers you, but for their sake so that they can grow.

To correct mistakes you need authority and love. Authority and love seem to be contradictory, but in reality they are not. Authority without love is stifling. Love without authority is shallow. A friend needs to have both authority and love, but they need to be in the right combination. This can happen if you are totally dispassionate and centered. When you allow room for mistakes, you can be both authoritative and sweet. That is how the Divine is, the right balance of both. Krishna and Jesus had both. Don't make a mistake by pointing out mistakes!

Once a lady came to me and said her husband had lied to her. She was very upset. I asked, "Why does your husband lie to you? Because he loves you, and is afraid to lose your love or hurt you. If he did not love you, he wouldn't lie to you!"

Do not tell a person a mistake he knows he has committed. By doing this, you will only make him feel more guilty. A magnanimous person will not pick on the mistakes of others and make them feel guilty; he will correct them with compassion and care.

16. Don't look for perfection

$\mathscr{M}$any a time, you become angry or miserable because of the feverishness for perfection.

If you are too much of a perfectionist, you are bound to be an angry person.

In a state of ignorance, imperfection is natural and perfection is an effort. In a state of wisdom or enlightenment, imperfection is an effort; perfection is a compulsion and is unavoidable! Perfection is taking total responsibility, and total responsibility means knowing that you are the only responsible person in the whole world. When you think that others are responsible, then your degree of responsibility diminishes. When you are in total 'vairagya' (dispassion), you can take care of even insignificant things with such perfection. Perfection is the very nature of the Enlightened One. When we are joyful, we don't look for perfection. If you are looking for perfection then you are not at the source of joy. Joy is the realisation that there is no vacation from wisdom. The world appears imperfect on the surface but, underneath, all is perfect. Perfection hides; imperfection shows off. The wise will not stay on the surface but will probe into the depth. Things are not blurred; your vision is blurred. Infinite actions prevail in the wholeness of consciousness, and yet the consciousness remains perfect, untouched. Realise this now and be natural.

In this world, everything cannot be perfect all the time. Even the best, the greatest of actions, performed with the noblest of intentions, will have some imperfections. It is but natural. Unfortunately, the tendency of our mind is to grab the imperfection and hold on to it. And, in the process, we end up making our moods, our minds imperfect and our souls reel with this nonsense. It is imperative to get out of these cycles, and to become strong and courageous from within.

17. Let us be unpredictable

We often behave like machines. A compliment makes us smile and an insult makes us frown. We don't have to react in the same way always. You have the freedom to respond differently. You don't have to answer all questions posed to you. As people have a right to question, you have the right whether to answer or not.

So, be unpredictable!

18. Have a sense of humour

$\mathcal{Y}$ou are endowed with certain naughtiness as a child. Keep it alive. Humour will grease all tough situations. One who has humour can sail through any conflict. Humour is the buffer that saves you from humiliation. If you refuse to be humiliated, you become invincible. Humour brings everyone together, while humiliation tears them apart. In a society torn with humiliation and insult, humour is like a breath of fresh air. Humour should be coupled with care and concern. Humour can keep the spirit high, yet if overdone it leaves a bad taste. Humour without wisdom is shallow. Humour without sensitivity is satire-it comes back to you with more problems.

The wise use humour to bring wisdom and to lighten situations. The intelligent use humour as a shield against humiliation. The cruel use humour as a sword to insult others. The irresponsible use humour to escape from responsibility. And fools take humour too seriously!

How does one cultivate a sense of humor? Humour is not just

words, it is the lightness of your being. You do not have to read and repeat jokes.

• Taking life not too seriously (because you will never come out of it alive)!

• Having a sense of belongingness with everybody, including those who are not friendly.

• Practicing yoga and meditation.

• Having unshakable faith in the Divine and in the laws of karma.

• Being in the company of those who live in knowledge and are humorous.

• A willingness to be a clown.

19. Don't be afraid to make mistakes

Whenever a boundary is broken, it creates some fear. The fear creates dislike. This dislike puts us back in the boundary. And to keep yourself in the boundary you put forth defenses. When you try to defend your position, it is such a stress. Every time you try to defend your position, it makes you more and more weak. Drop all your defenses. When you are totally defenseless, that's when you'll be strong.

Your knowledge of a mistake comes to you when you are innocent! Whatever mistake has happened, do not consider yourself a sinner because in the present moment you are again new, pure and clear. Mistakes of the past are past. When this knowledge comes, you are again perfect. Often, mothers scold their children and afterwards feel so guilty.

Okay, you got angry at your kid once or twice. Why? Because of the lack of awareness!

Awareness was missing, so the anger came up. Knowledge of the self, truth and skills can bring out the best in you. So, don't be afraid to make mistakes, but not the same mistakes. You have got to be innovative even in your mistakes!

20. Overcome your prejudice

Your prejudice against gender, religion, caste and class does not allow you to mingle with everyone around you. Often, you don't sit with people who are not economically or socially at par with you. You have to learn to break that barrier. Also, there is age prejudice. Teenagers don't like to have fun with elderly people and vice versa. Gender prejudice is more prevalent in rural areas. Caste system is present even among the royalties of Europe, the UK and Japan.

Religious prejudice is well known. There are good people and bad people in every community, religion and every section of society. Don't be prejudiced against them. At the same time don't be shy about your identity. When you overcome prejudice, you will be very natural, and your quality of life will improve.

21. Feel that "I am blessed"

There is so much talk about success. Have you ever thought what success is? Success is simply ignorance about one's capabilities. Success is ignorance about the power of the self. Because you assume you can do only this much. If there are obstacles, you are clear about your objective. With a calm and serene mind, think of many possibilities. Know that failures are stepping stones for greater success. Actually, there are no failures in life.

All the seeming failures are only stepping stones for greater success. If you feel the obstacle is too much, deep prayer can work miracles.

The feeling that "I am blessed" can help you overcome any failure. Once you realise that you are blessed, then all the complaints disappear, all the grumbling disappears, all the insecurities disappear, a sense of not being loved disappears, wanting love disappears.

Ego is always ambitious and wants to do tough jobs like climbing Mount Everest.

Whereas in a simple act like watching a butterfly, watering the garden, watching the birds or the sky, can bring deep relaxation, and relaxation connects you with your source.

Seemingly trivial actions open a new dimension and bring in immense peace and rest. Just come out of your little shell and feel free.

There is a saying: 'Behind every successful man is a woman'. I will modify this: Behind every success there is the Divine saying 'I am behind you'.

22. Do random acts of kindness

*A*biding in the self you become the valentine for the whole world. Spirit is the valentine of matter, and matter is the valentine of spirit. They are made for each other. They uphold each other. If you do not respect the spirit, then matter is not pleased. If you honour the spirit then you will care for the world, and when you care for the world it will take care of you.

You are the Christmas tree. At the time of year when no tree bears anything, it has many gifts to offer. A Christmas tree bears the gifts and the lights not for itself. Similarly, all the gifts you are carrying in your life are for others. Anyone who comes to you, you offer them your gifts. When you show kindness, your true nature comes into play. Have you ever done acts of kindness without expecting anything out of it?

Our service should not be mechanical. Once some boy scouts were at a sunday service, when the priest said, "You should serve." They asked, "What is this service? Could you give us some example?" He said, "Suppose an old woman wants to cross a road, go and help her cross the road."

So the boys went and looked for a whole week, but there was no old woman trying to cross a street. Finally, four of them found a woman walking on a footpath. One of the boys went and asked her, "Madam, would you like to cross the road?" She turned and said, "No." He was disappointed. So another boy went and asked her again, thinking, perhaps, that the first boy hadn't asked properly. The woman was now a little bit confused. She wondered why she was being asked this. So, she said, it was all right for him to take her across the road. Once they had reached the other side, a third boy came and asked her, "Would you like to cross the road?" Now it really bothered her. When the fourth one approached her, she almost screamed and ran away!

You don't have to plan acts of kindness. Just do something spontaneously. When you do random acts of kindness, you come in touch with your true nature.

23. Be a student, always

*K*now that you are a student forever. Do not underestimate anybody. Knowledge may come to you from any corner. Remember the ancient saying "let knowledge flow to me from all sides". Each occasion teaches you and each person teaches you. The world is your teacher. When you are always looking to learn, you will stop underestimating others. Humility will dawn in your life.

There is a nice story. A man earned a lot of money and then gave all his property to his son. The son then built a small house behind his big house and told his parents: "Now you have to stay there." So the old couple stayed there, while the son and his family lived in the bungalow. One day, while playing, the grandchild came to his grandfather's home, where everything was in pathetic condition. The grandchild said,

"Grandpa, be careful with your plate and chair. Don't break them."

When he asked why, the child said, "Because tomorrow, my father will need them." One does not realise this fact. You are also going to be old one day.

24. Dream the impossible

THE ART OF LIVING

*U*nless you have a dream, you cannot realise it. Every invention has come out of a dream. Dream the impossible. Obviously, dreaming employs something which is beyond your perceived capacity.

Consider the faculty which is the preceptor of the dream. Some dreams have impacted your daily living and others have not. Some dreams you remember, and others you have forgotten.

We are all born in this world to do something wonderful and unique; don't let this opportunity pass by. Give yourself the freedom to dream and think big. Have the courage and determination to achieve those dreams that are dear to you. Many a time people who dreamt big were ridiculed, but they remained strong to achieve their goals.

Do something creative. Not a year should pass without doing something creative.

25. Compare your performance

*A*s we flip the calendar, we need to keep flipping our mind as well. Often, our diaries are full with memories. See that you don't fill your future dates with past events. Allow the space for creativity to dawn. Celebration of the New Year allows you to be wise. Learn and unlearn from the past, and move on. In the past year, how many days were you in sanyas? How many days were you struggling, being caught in maya? Turn back and remember the whole year. Do not run away from anything. Do not reject anything. Do not go away from anything. At the same time, let your attention be on the self. This is a delicate balance. That balance is yoga.

A poor man celebrates the New Year once a year. A rich man celebrates each day. But the richest man celebrates every moment.

How rich are you? If you celebrate every moment, you are the Lord of Creation. Review the year while you celebrate. This is your homework. Compare your performance in the year before last and smile. This year is fortunate because you are living at this time!!!

When you are living for the sake of the world, the world is fortunate. Let time celebrate your presence. You keep smiling as ever.

When you let time celebrate you, you are a witness amid celebration. The heart always longs for the old, the mind for the new. Life is a combination of both. Let the New Year bring into our life ancient wisdom and modernity, as life is incomplete without either of them. Don't feel shy to speak about human and spiritual values. The time has come now to call the whole world!

Be ever new, happy you!!!!

The Art of Living
&
The International Association for Human Values

Transforming Lives

The Founder
His Holiness Sri Sri Ravi Shankar

His Holiness Sri Sri Ravi Shankar has been instrumental in enabling millions from every walk of life, lead lives that are happier, fuller, healthier and stress-free. He has been feted the world over by governments and the common man alike. He is the founder of the Art of Living, spread across 151 countries today, and the International Association for Human Values, headquartered in Geneva. Through His organisations, His Holiness revives human values, promotes global peace and guides comprehensive service and development endeavours that transform lives all over the globe.

In a world fraught with conflict, His message that all individuals, societies, civilizations, cultures, religions and spiritual traditions share common human values has deeply resonated everywhere, with a power and gentleness that are uniquely exuded by H. H. Sri Sri Ravi Shankar Himself. He inspires sustained individual commitment to joyful living, selfless service and self-awareness through His eternal message of peace, love and seva (service). He has addressed diverse audiences, including Heads of State, the United Nations, the World Economic Forum, scientists, legislators and various parliaments, political and business leaders, academic and social institutions and other decision-makers etc. The innumerable awards and honours conferred upon His Holiness reflect the extent and depths of gratitude felt for his inspiration, wisdom and presence.

Yet, beyond all these immense, visible, tangible achievements, He is a Guru whose touch is personal. He has always maintained that we are here to develop the individual, not a movement. He lights the flame of love in one heart; this one heart transforms another ten and these in turn transform hundred more. He creates opportunities for leadership and service for every single person connected with him. His compassion, joy, love, wisdom and playfulness have given a whole new dimension to spirituality.

Born on May 13 1956, in Papanasam (Tamil Nadu, India), His Holiness Sri Sri Ravi Shankar was often found rapt in meditation as a little boy. By the time He was four, He was already reciting the Bhagwad Gita and other scriptures. As a young boy, He would often tell His friends, "People all over the world are waiting for me." By seventeen, He had completed His education in both Vedic literature and modern science.

In 1982, H. H. Sri Sri Ravi Shankar began teaching the Sudarshan Kriya, a powerful, yet simple breathing technique that eliminates stress and brings one into the present moment completely. This is taught around the world as part of the Art of Living Programmes, benefiting and healing innumerable people in various ways.

The Art of Living
In Service Around The World

The largest volunteer-based network in the world, with a wide range of social, cultural and spiritual activities, the Art of Living has reached out, since 1982, to over 20 million people from all walks of life. A non-profit, educational and humanitarian organization, it is committed to creating peace from the level of the individual upwards, and fostering human values within the global community. Currently, the Art of Living service projects and educational programmes are carried out in over 151 countries. The organisation works in special consultative status with the Economic and Social Council (ECOSOC) of the United Nations, participating in a variety of committees and activities related to health and conflict resolution.

(www.artofliving.org)

The Art of Living
Stress Elimination Programmes

Holistic Development of Body, Mind & Spirit

The Art of Living programmes are a combination of the best of ancient wisdom and modern science. They cater to every age group - children, youth, adults - and every section of the society – rural communities, governments, corporate houses, etc. Emphasizing holistic living and personal self-development, the programmes facilitate the complete blossoming of an individual's full potential. The cornerstone of all our workshops is the Sudarshan Kriya, a unique and powerful breathing practice.

The Art of Living Course Part I

The Art of Living Course Part I is a simple, yet profound programme that offers the Sudarshan Kriya, practical spiritual knowledge, deep meditation and interactive processes. The Sudarshan Kriya is a unique breathing exercise introduced by His Holiness Sri Sri Ravi Shankar.

It is the cornerstone of all Art of Living Programmes. A powerful energiser that cleanses deep-rooted physical, mental and emotional stresses and toxins, it helps to synchronise the mind and body with the rhythms of nature.

Serenity, centeredness, better health, more harmonious relationships and greater joy and enthusiasm for life are just some of the benefits of this course.

The Art of Living Course Part II

The Art of Living Course Part II takes one deeper into one's self. Very often, one takes a vacation, only to return feeling more exhausted and in need of another one! The Part II course is a vacation, in the true sense of the word, leaving one rejuvenated and relaxed, both physically and mentally. It includes Sadhana (spiritual practices), Satsang (spiritual communion through singing), Seva (service) and Silence.

Sahaj Samadhi Meditation

The Sahaj Samadhi Meditation is a delightfully simple, yet powerful process that allows one to experience the depth of the Being. Through this ancient, natural and graceful system of meditation, the mind settles down.

THE ART OF LIVING

It lets goes of all stresses and tensions, and centres itself in the present moment, enabling one to experience profound silence and inner bliss.

Divya Samaaj ka Nirmaan (DSN)

A society is a reflection of its individuals, and the DSN empowers an individual to contribute positively to his or her society. Divya Samaaj ka Nirmaan (DSN) literally means "Creating a divine society." If you've ever asked yourself, "What can I do to make this world a better place?", then DSN is your answer.

The All Round Training in Excellence (ART Excel)
(for 8-14 year olds)

The ART Excel is tailor-made for our young ones. It is a highly effective programme that positively shapes the lives of children. It helps release stress and overcome emotions like fear, anger, aggression, shyness etc., through breathing. The programme develops concentration, builds confidence and inculcates human values, such as sharing, caring, acceptance, trust and respect, through interactive games and various processes.

The Youth Empowerment Seminar (YES)

(for 15-21 year olds)

In an age where young adults grapple with peer pressure and stiff academic competition, the YES programme enables youth to excel by equipping them to handle their minds and emotions positively. It inculcates a sense of belongingness and instills leadership skills. Through the Sudarshan Kriya, interactive processes, discussions and games, students benefit from improved memory, concentration, clarity, creativity and confidence.

The Prison Programme

The Prison Programme addresses the needs of prison inmates, as well as those individuals and institutions that combat crime and violence. The techniques release stress and help reduce violent tendencies and drug dependence. The life skill imparted in the Programme enables inmates accept responsibility for their past actions and successfully handle future conflict or stressful situations. The aim is to facilitate genuine rehabilitation so that the inmates are truly able to make a fresh, new and happy beginning.

The Corporate Executive Programme (CEP)

The Corporate Executive Programme, also called the APEX (Achieving Personal Excellence) Programme, is highly specialized, practical and effective. It presents a paradigm shift from "working hard" to "working smart". It enables employees to strike a balance between meeting the demands of their personal life and professional commitments. The programme strengthens managers and employees, enabling them to experience unshakable calm and inner clarity in the face of any business challenge or crisis. In the corporate world, only the fittest survive and the CEP ensures maximum fitness at every level.

Sri Sri Yoga

Sri Sri Yoga brings us the wisdom and techniques of yoga in a joyful, pure and in-depth system. Asanas, Pranayamas and Meditation are the main aspects of this programme. It unites body, spirit and mind through the breath. It presents us with peace, joy, increased concentration, greater energy and enthusiasm, enhanced flexibility and strength, regulation of digestive and other systems, weight loss as well as other benefits.

(www.srisriyoga.in)

The International Association for Human Values (IAHV)

The International Association for Human Values (IAHV) was founded in Geneva in 1997 to foster, on a global scale, a deeper understanding of the values that unite us as a single human community. Its vision is to celebrate distinct traditions and diversity while simultaneously creating a greater understanding and appreciation of our many shared principles. To this end, the IAHV develops and promotes programmes that generate awareness and encourage the practice of human values in everyday life. It advocates that the incorporation of human values in all aspects of life will ultimately lead to harmony amidst diversity and the development of a more peaceful, just and sustainable world. The IAHV works in collaboration with partners dedicated to similar goals, including governments, multilateral agencies, educational institutions, NGOs, corporations and individuals.

(www.iahv.org)

Service Projects

Sustainable Rural Development

With the objective of social and economic reliance, both at the individual and community level, this Art of Living Programme works at holistically strengthening and empowering communities worldwide, at the grassroots level, by addressing the needs of the rural communities' poor and disadvantaged. It achieves this through a variety of programmes, like the Sri Sri Rural Development Programme (SSRDP), the Youth Leadership Training Programme (YLTP) and the 5H Programme (where the 5Hs are Health, Hygiene, Homes, Human Values and Harmony amidst Diversity). Hundreds of thousands, the world over, have benefited from these Programmes.

(www.5h.org)

Organic Farming

The Art of Living is taking concrete and substantial steps to revive traditional and efficient agricultural practices like organic (chemical-free) farming, which consequently brings prosperity and joy to the farming community. It also runs the Sri Sri Mobile Agricultural Institute (SSMAI) which brings agriculture-related knowledge right to the farmers' doorsteps, thereby instilling self-confidence in them.

Trauma Relief

From an earthquake in Iran to a tsunami in Sri Lanka, from floods in Germany to cyclones in India, from wars in Iraq and Croatia to a school-massacre in Russia, from strife in Bosnia and Afghanistan, to 9/11 in the USA, Art of Living volunteers, the world over, have come together over the years, whenever tragedy has struck our planet, to answer the cry for help in a unanimous spirit of service and solidarity, irrespective of caste, creed, religion or geography.

Peace Initiatives

In a world suffering from intolerance, insecurity, doubt and conflict, His Holiness Sri Sri Ravi Shankar leads the way in extending invitations of friendship and peace. His unrelenting commitment to build bridges between estranged communities and to help people overcome the trauma of conflict paves the way for mutual trust and lasting peace. The Art of Living has been working to promote friendly ties within and between several

THE ART OF LIVING

regions, including Afghanistan, Kosovo, Pakistan, Israel, Lebanon, Nepal and Kashmir (India), with the aim of attaining peace and rapid economic development.

Education

The Art of Living is committed to making free-of-cost quality education accessible to the poor, thereby providing a joyful and inspiring learning environment to children from urban, rural and tribal areas. A range of schools, offering value-based education, have been set up: Tribal Schools, Rural Schools, Sri Sri Seva Mandirs (for children from slums, or urban low-income areas), the Ashram School (catering to first generation learners from the villages surrounding the Bangalore International Centre), Vedic/Agama Schools (reviving traditional Vedic knowledge) and Sri Sri Ravi Shankar Vidya Mandirs (catering to higher income groups). The organisation also runs institutions of higher education. (www.srisrischools.net)

Women Empowerment

The Art of Living runs Programmes aimed at uplifting women in the poorest villages of the world. The mission is to transform the lives of women and girls, who are illiterate, emotionally abused and often afflicted with serious health problems. The organisation imparts basic literacy skills and vocational training, facilitating self-sufficiency. In addition, they are made aware of hygiene, and are taught yoga and meditation. The increase in their self-respect and dignity is immeasurable. One such programme running in Urugalli (a village in Karnataka, India) is VISTA (Value Integrated Services to All).

Drug Addiction Rehabilitation

Through its programmes, the Art of Living has been working with victims of drug abuse; both on its own as well as in partnership with other organizations. The aim is to aid drug-addicts to completely overcome their drug dependence, thereby facilitating true rehabilitation.

International Centres

INDIA
21st KM, Kanakapura Road, Udayapura
Bangalore – 560 082, Karnataka
Telephone   : 91-80-28432273, 74
Fax   : 91-80-28432832
Email   : info@vvmvp.org

CANADA
Box 170-13 Infinity Road
St. Mathieu-du-Parc, Quebec, G0X 1N0
Telephone   : 819-532-3328
Fax   : 819-532-2033
Email   : artofliving.northeast@sympatico.ca

GERMANY
Bad Antogast 1, 77728 Oppenau
Telephone   : 0049 7804-910 923
Fax   : 0049 7804-910 924
Email   : artofliving.germany@t-online.de

• www.srisriravishankar.org • www.artofliving.org
• www.iahv.org • www.5h.org